MW01051580

STUNTPEOPLE

BY
Gail Stewart

EDITED BY
Anita Larsen

KENNETH G. PARKER ELEM. SCHOOL
MEDIA CENTER
IND. SCHOOL DIST. #728
ELK RIVER, MINNESOTA

PUBLISHED BY
CRESTWOOD HOUSE
Mankato, MN, U.S.A.

CIP

LIBRARY OF CONGRESS CATALOGING IN PUBLICATION DATA

Stewart, Gail.
  Stuntpeople.

  (At risk)
  Includes index.
  SUMMARY: Describes the job of being a stunt performer, examining the history, techniques, and tools of the occupation.
  1. Stunt men and women—Juvenile literature. [1. Stunt men and women. 2. Occupations.] I. Larsen, Anita. II Title. III. Series.
PN1995.9.S7S74 1988   791.43′028—dc19   88-14946
ISBN 0-89686-396-4

International Standard
Book Number:
0-89686-396-4

Library of Congress
Catalog Card Number:
88-14946

PHOTO CREDITS

Cover: Globe Photos, Inc.: Gene Trindl
Academy of Motion Picture Arts & Sciences: (© Simon Productions) 4; (© 1959 Loew's, Inc.) 15; (© 1978 Warner Bros. Inc. All Rights Reserved.) 7, 41
Globe Photos, Inc.: (John R. Hamilton) 8, 16, 21, 22; (Bob Noble) 27; (Dennis Barna) 29; (Gene Trindl) 39; (Phil Stern) 24, 25, 26; (Jack Hamilton) 30, 31, 32, 33, 36
Photofile: (T. Tracy) 12
Jeroboam, Inc.: 19
Wide World Photos, Inc.: (Bob Galbraith) 42-43

Copyright © 1988 by Crestwood House, Inc. All rights reserved. No part of this book may be reproduced in any form without written permission from the publisher, except for brief passages included in a review. Printed in the United States of America.

Produced by Carnival Enterprises.

CRESTWOOD HOUSE

Box 3427, Mankato, MN, U.S.A. 56002

TABLE OF CONTENTS

*Being a stuntperson requires training and skill—stuntpeople are
not just daredevils.*

4

THE CHASE...

The car turned the corner quickly. The driver looked in his rear view mirror. Were the two men following him? He remembered how frightening they looked and shuddered.

Suddenly a van appeared behind him. Its headlights glared in his mirror. The killers—it had to be them! He pushed down hard on the gas pedal. The needle on the speedometer climbed to 45... 50...55.

But the van stayed with him. It was close enough now so that he could see the two men in the front seat. They would kill him if they caught him, he was sure of that.

He jerked the steering wheel hard to the left. The car's tires screeched as they tried to grip the wet pavement. The accelerator was touching the floor now—65...70...80. He headed toward the bridge.

Without warning, a truck pulled out of a driveway. The speeding car swerved, missing the truck by inches. A flashing sign ahead warned of bridge repair. There was no way he could stop!

His car hit a jagged piece of broken concrete and lurched through the air. Still in midair, it clipped the side of a parked car and spun out of control. The car landed at the edge of the bridge, teetering half on, half off.

There was no sign of the van now. The man's only

enemies were the smoke and flames coming from the car and the icy water below him. He was dazed from the accident, but he knew he had to get out of the car before it exploded.

He looked down at the black water 40 feet below. There was no choice—no chance to think. He had to jump and pray that the teetering car wouldn't fall in on top of him.

Pushing the car door open, he leaped. As he hit the icy water, the car above him exploded into clouds of fire and smoke.

"Okay, good!" yells a voice. "Print that one. Good job, Bill!"

The man who, moments before, had leaped into the water to escape certain death, smiled broadly. He swam quickly to the shore and climbed up on the bank. An assistant was waiting for him with a big, warm towel and a cup of coffee.

Bill is a stuntman—one of a small group of people who make their living "doubling," or filling in, for the actors. Stunt doubles like Bill are experts at doing dangerous work without getting hurt. They may be needed to fall out of a window, roll a car, get shot off a galloping horse, or worse.

But whatever they do, they must "pretend" to be the actor. They wear the same clothes and a wig, if necessary. And if they do their job well, the audience never notices!

Some people might think stuntpeople are

Stuntpeople practice their "gags" to make them as safe as possible.

daredevils—just out for thrills. That isn't true at all. Their job requires training and skill. Each stunt, or "gag," as it is called, is carefully planned down to the smallest detail.

The stuntperson controls the danger by making the gag as safe as it can possibly be. This job has a strong element of danger, but stuntpeople say the danger only makes the job more interesting!

7

THE EARLIEST STUNTPEOPLE

Back in William Shakespeare's day, in 16th century England, there were plenty of exciting battles in many of the plays performed. Swordfights were especially plentiful, and audiences loved them. Of course the actors in these stage plays had to do their own stunts. No tricks could be played with cameras. There was a demand for actors who could make a pretend swordfight look real.

Audiences then were not easily fooled. They often saw public demonstrations of the king's swordsmen. They knew what good swordplay looked like. An actor who waved a sword around without knowing

In early films actors did their own stunts.

what he was doing would be laughed at or booed off the stage. It's no wonder that the most popular actors of the day were also some of the finest swordsmen in England!

SILENT FILMS

The first movies, made in the early 1900s, are often called "silent films." That's because the technology for putting sound together with film didn't exist. Most theaters hired someone to play the piano during the film to provide background music. The early films depended more on action rather than words. These were visual things an audience could understand without sound.

Most of the silent films had lots of action—good guys and bad guys and lots of chases and fights. Just as in the 16th century, early movie actors did their own stunts. Most of the popular actors of the day had been circus performers or rodeo riders.

In a circus or rodeo, dangerous stunts were simply part of a day's work. When these performers began working in films, no one seemed surprised if a director needed someone to fall off a horse or jump off a speeding train. An actor did it, no questions asked.

Helen Gibson was one of the early actors in silent films. She had made her mark as a rider in a Wild

West show before becoming a film star. In 1915, Helen thrilled moviegoers with her famous motorcycle stunt. Traveling at full speed on the cycle, she chased a runaway freight train. She crashed through a wooden gate and went up a platform into a train station. Sailing into the air, she and her speeding motorcycle landed on a flatcar of the passing train!

TALKIES

Then came "talkies," films where you could actually hear the actors. Audiences loved talkies, and silent films became a thing of the past.

There were other changes that came with talkies, too. More types of movies could be made. Talkies didn't *have* to be non-stop action to interest movie audiences. Film studios made dramas that had lots of dialogue, or conversation, between actors. This often called for actors with good voices as well as physical ability. As one early film director remembers, "To get a big part in talkies, an actor had to do more than just prove he could fall off a stagecoach without killing himself!" Many of the old circus and rodeo performers found themselves out of work.

Some silent film stars were dropped for other reasons. One of the popular Western actors in silent films was Yakima Canutt. Canutt had made it as a rodeo star, busting broncos before becoming an actor in cowboy movies. He had the acting ability to continue in talkies, but the wrong voice! A bad case of flu when he was a child had left him with a gravelly, hoarse-sounding voice. Many other performers were dropped because their voices didn't sound right for the parts they would play.

But while Yakima Canutt and other ex-rodeo, ex-circus performers were no longer starring in movies, many of them found a new role to play. The talkies brought the rise of the stuntperson to Hollywood.

ACT, BUT DON'T HURT YOURSELF!

Why didn't actors keep doing their own stunts as they had in silent films? The easiest answer is simply that they had no experience in performing stunts. These actors were not the same people who had been trained to perform dangerous acts. They had no interest in being dragged by a team of wild horses or getting punched in the mouth and knocked down in a movie fight.

Another reason stuntpeople became more common is that movie studios were anxious to protect stars. Without experience and training, an actor could be seriously injured or even killed doing

Action-packed Westerns created a demand for stuntpeople.

12

a stunt.

Besides, the studios had their own financial interests to look out for. Every day of shooting a picture cost money. Having the leading actor in a hospital when a movie was half-done could be expensive. It was far easier to hire a stuntperson and pay him or her $5 a day!

COWBOYS AND THEIR HORSES

Audiences just couldn't get enough of cowboy movies. The popular "blood and thunder" Westerns, as they were called, included lots of shooting and stunts with horses. Yakima Canutt and a few other ex-rodeo riders had all the work they could handle.

But moviegoers got impatient with seeing the same old action scenes. More and more movies were made every year, and film producers realized that they couldn't keep doing the same stunts. Audiences wanted more danger, more thrills. The demand for stuntpeople grew.

One spectacular stunt, invented and performed by Canutt in a 1938 movie called *Riders of the Dawn,* was the "stagecoach transfer." Canutt had to move at full gallop from his horse onto a stagecoach that was also going full speed. When he got to the stagecoach, he had to fight with "the bad guy" for a while, and then was pushed forward onto the backs of the horses. He fell between them onto the ground. As the stagecoach passed over him, he grabbed the rear axle and was dragged along the ground. After much struggling, he was able to climb back onto the rear of the stagecoach, creep over the roof, and jump on "the bad guy" again. What a day's work!

No one believed such a gag could be done without any camera tricks at all. Yakima Canutt showed what could be done with courage, imagination, and careful planning. Film makers of the '80s are still using Canutt's ideas for modern stunts. The famous stagecoach transfer was done—using a truck instead of a stagecoach—in *Raiders of the Lost Ark.*

Sometimes directors asked too much of their stuntpeople, maybe because they weren't as concerned about safety. Or sometimes they misjudged the danger involved. Whatever the reason, many stuntpeople were killed in the early days of motion pictures.

Horses, too, were injured and killed. In the first version of the movie *Ben Hur,* made in the 1920s, there was an exciting chariot race. The directors wanted that scene to look as real as possible. They encouraged the stuntpeople to run a real race and said they'd award cash prizes to the winners. From greed or carelessness, the drivers ran many animals too hard. More than 130 horses died as a result of that one scene in *Ben Hur.* In 1958, Hollywood did a

During its filming, **Ben Hur** *used many horses and stuntpeople.*

remake of the film. By this time, laws had been passed that set guidelines and limits for the use of animals in films. Who arranged all the stunts for the chariot race in the 1958 version of *Ben Hur*? Yakima Canutt! No horses were killed in that race.

Another hazard to horses that has been eliminated was a device called a "Running W." Film makers would use a Running W when the scene called for a horse to fall. A cable would pull the horse's legs out from under him.

Today, horses are trained to fall at a signal from the stuntperson. The ground where the fall will be taken is made soft and spongy to reduce the chances of serious injury to horse and rider.

DON'T LEAN FORWARD!

Fistfights on camera haven't changed all that much since the early days of film. Stuntpeople call them "light gags," meaning that they aren't too dangerous. Still stuntmen have received broken jaws, noses, and teeth by not being careful.

Fights in the movies or on television are carefully planned. Every swing, step, stagger, and fall is practiced over and over.

Camera angles are extremely important, too. In a perfectly done fight gag, none of the punches really lands! The trick is to position the camera directly behind the fighter. He or she throws a punch across the other's face. The important thing is that word "across." The punch goes from side to side, and the camera can't really tell how far away from the person's face the punch goes. The person who's getting "hit" snaps his head back, maybe staggering a little for a realistic effect.

After the filming is over, sound effects of punches and grunts are added to make it seem even more real. It sounds easy, but any stuntperson can tell you it takes practice to get it right.

Fight scenes in movies are well-practiced—and realistic!

CANDY GLASS AND OTHER ILLUSIONS

How many times have you seen an actor jump or thrown through a window? As we watch him crashing through the glass, we wince. All that sharp glass! How does the stuntperson manage to avoid getting cut?

Actually, it's not really glass at all. It is called "candy glass," although it isn't made from candy anymore. In the 30s and 40s, film makers made fake glass out of sugar and hot water. It tasted pretty good. But it also tended to melt under the bright lights needed for the cameras.

So a better kind of fake glass was invented. This was plastic that snapped into many pieces when it was touched. This new candy glass is also safer for the stuntperson. When it shatters, there are no razor-sharp points that might penetrate skin and eyes.

Candy glass is one of the little "helps" a stuntperson needs to make the gag safer. These helps are called "props," and some of them are clever.

Much of the furniture thrown during fight scenes is made of balsa wood. This wood is extremely light and reduces the chance of injury. Also, real nails are never used to connect the parts of furniture. Pieces are glued together. When Actor A picks up a table and smashes it over Actor B's head, it is the table and

Out of view of the camera, an airbag is ready to catch a cowboy.

not the head that is destroyed!

Sometimes in one of these fights, one fighter breaks a board over someone else's head. That, too, is balsa wood. But balsa wood can still leave a nasty bump. One more step is needed. The person in charge of props, called the special effects advisor, will saw the board almost in half so it breaks easily.

BLOOD AND MORE BLOOD

A fight often needs blood to be realistic. In the old days, the audience believed that ketchup squirted on the hero's clothes was real blood. But modern film makers use lots of better tricks, and they enjoy using them. "It's almost a challenge to see how realistic we can be," said one stuntperson. "How believable can a camera shooting get? Sometimes when they get me hooked up to all the knives and blood bags, and I see what I look like afterwards, I almost believe it happened to me!"

Film makers achieve those gruesome effects in a couple of different ways. The first is by using an air gun. This device actually shoots tiny sacs of fake blood at the actor. When the blood hits skin or clothing, it looks to the camera—and the viewers— as though the character had been shot.

Before filming begins, two stuntmen practice their "gag" one more time.

Another more realistic way is by using powder charges called "squibs." These are taped to small metal plates that are sewn into the stuntperson's clothing. Tiny sacs of fake blood are taped to the squibs. When the powder charge goes off, the sac breaks, and it looks as though the stuntperson was bleeding.

Sometimes the story calls for the character to bleed from the mouth during a fight. Then the stuntperson hides a fake blood capsule in his mouth. A blood capsule is about the same size and shape as a vitamin capsule, except it's softer. When the stuntperson bites down his mouth fills with fake blood. Fake blood is made from red food dye and corn syrup and is safe to eat.

21

FALLS, BAGS, AND BOXES

Every stuntperson must know how to fall. Sometimes the falls are spectacular—from hundreds of feet up. But most common are "short" falls, usually under 20 feet. Any stuntperson will tell you that falls, no matter from what height, can be dangerous.

Whenever there is a fall, the stuntperson needs a "catcher"—something to land on that will cushion the fall a little. For "short" falls, cardboard boxes are used. Sometimes several boxes are stacked on top of one another. Once in a while, matresses are stacked between the boxes. This gives the stuntperson extra protection.

Even a fall considered "short" by stunting standards can critically injure someone if it's done incorrectly. For instance, it's important not to land on your side. That can jam the knees together and cause serious injuries. Most often, a stuntperson likes to finish a fall by landing on his shoulder and rolling. That takes stress off the back and neck.

For a fall of more than 20 feet, stuntpeople use "airbags," two bags made of thick plastic, one inside the other. The double bag idea is to provide a cushion of air between the bags. That protects the stuntperson a little more from the hard ground below. Airbags

The airbags, camera crew, and stuntperson are ready—roll 'em!

A stuntperson needs courage to jump blindly from a helicopter.

come in different sizes—from 3 by 5 feet up to 50 by 100 feet.

Even with catchers, falling presents a problem. It's against human instinct to jump blindly into empty space, and that's what stuntpeople often have to do.

In some scenes the airbag may be hidden. The story may call for the jump to be made in darkness. But any hesitation—even a split-second stop to look for an airbag target—can be picked up by the camera. If it doesn't look real, the director will yell "Cut!" and the stunt will have to be redone.

Even a split-second hesitation in a jumping stunt can be picked up by the camera.

DAR ROBINSON: "THE BEST IN THE BUSINESS"

The best stuntperson ever—in terms of high falls—was a man named Dar Robinson. Robinson had worked as a stuntman for 19 years before he was killed in a motorcycle accident during the filming of a movie. He did high falls no one could believe—especially other stuntpeople.

One fall was 311 feet from a helicopter! His target

KENNETH G. PARKER ELEM. SCHOOL
MEDIA CENTER
IND. SCHOOL DIST. #728
ELK RIVER, MINNESOTA

If it doesn't look real, the stunt will have to be done again.

was a 24 by 28-foot airbag. To make the stunt even more difficult, the helicopter couldn't stop over the airbag. Air movement from the helicopter blade—even from that far up—would have blown the target around. Without perfect timing, Dar Robinson faced death.

How did Robinson know exactly when to jump? He was a very careful stuntman. He spent hours with a calculator, pencil, and paper going over every detail of every stunt. He had a dummy that was made identical to his height and weight and with all sorts of scientific instruments attached. The dummy's name was George.

Dar Robinson was one of the best stuntpeople who ever lived.

Before actually making any high fall, Robinson had George do it first. Then he examined George and his various instruments. That gave him information on how to do the gag safely himself.

It was a good thing he had George, because when first testing that helicopter jump, George fell and completely missed the airbag! Robinson did some quick calculations about the speed of the helicopter and the wind, and that helped him do it right.

Because Dar Robinson was one of the best, he was paid well for the stunts he did. Most stuntpeople are paid a certain fee each day—usually around $300. In addition, they are paid for each gag they perform. The harder the gag, the more money they earn. For one of his more difficult falls, Robinson would be paid a quarter of a million dollars!

One stunt Robinson performed was for the movie *High Point.* The story called for his character to fall off the tallest structure in the world—the Canadian National Tower in Toronto, Canada. The CN Tower stands 1,178 feet tall.

Obviously, no one could really fall that distance without killing himself. They made it look as though he really fell that far. With a special harness hidden under his clothes, and a thin cable attached to the harness, Robinson fell 900 feet, screaming all the way. The cable pulled tight, and Robinson dangled there until crew members rescued him. The feeling of leaping off that building must have been

Dar Robinson leaves a plane to complete another gag.

29

Dar jumps from the top of the Canadian National Tower.

As he nears the end of his jump...

...his leg harness breaks his fall and safely holds him.

Dar's crew removes him from his harness — another gag is successfully completed.

terrifying—especially knowing that a thin cable was his only lifeline!

After Robinson was killed, Burt Reynolds, who had used Robinson in several movies as a stuntman, said that Dar Robinson was one of the greatest of them all. "In terms of sheer courage," Reynolds said, "Dar had no peer."

CAR STUNTS

We've all seen exciting chase scenes in movies and on television. Did you know that a car chase involving two cars usually takes 10 or 12 cars? The chase is broken down into small parts, with a car doing one of those parts. The chase is then stopped, and cameras are set up farther down the road or around the corner. Another car, exactly like the first, then goes through its part of the chase.

Cars driven for stunts are rebuilt for extra safety. The roofs are lined with steel bars, which keep the roof from caving in during a roll-over. These special bars are called "roll bars." For very dangerous stunts, the insides of the cars have full steel cages. These are a lot like roll bars, except the cage goes all the way around the steering wheel, front seat, and front windows.

Another way stuntpeople make their cars safer is by removing all door and window handles that stick out. The regular gas tank is replaced with a small, unbreakable one made of plastic. This eliminates the danger of explosion or fire. There are also new shock absorbers and special tires and seat belts.

One gag commonly used is the roll. A roll is just what it sounds like. To get a car to roll over and over, a stuntman named Hal Needham invented what is called a "cannon ram." A miniature cannon is attached under the wheel of the car. A heavy pole is loaded into the cannon. The driver presses a button on his dashboard to set off an explosion. The pole fires down on the ground, pushing the car up on one side.

The first time a cannon ram was tried, it had a little too much force. The force of the cannon heaved the car almost 20 feet into the air, and it rolled over eight times! The driver had severe injuries to his back. The cannon has been made less dangerous now, but it still puts a lot of stress on the driver's back.

Another way of rolling a car is by using a ramp. The ramp is hidden from the camera. Most ramps are about 3 feet high and 12 or 15 feet long. The driver positions his car so that only the wheels on one side of the car are on the ramp. At the end of the ramp, he jerks his steering wheel sharply to the left or right. This sudden turn makes the car roll off the ramp.

Sometimes we see a spectacular shot of a car being driven off a cliff and exploding as it hits the ground below. To achieve this illusion, the stuntperson drives

Fire stunts are the most dangerous gags.

to the edge of the cliff. The car is then wired to a romote control device. When the cameras are ready, the car "drives" itself off the cliff. The stuntperson is safely outside the car.

PLAYING WITH FIRE

There are probably no stunts as dangerous as those involving fire. Some stuntpeople specialize in fire stunts, but there aren't many who honestly like the job. Special technology can protect a stuntperson from flames, but not from blistering heat.

Safety crews have to be present whenever a fire stunt is being done. They are armed with blankets and fire extinguishers to put out the fire quickly, the instant the scene is finished.

Once in a while, the fire burns too quickly, and the stuntperson knows he is in trouble. If that happens, he screams "Hit me!" That is the signal for the fire safety people to put out the fire, no matter how much of the scene is left to film.

For protection, a stuntperson must use either a special fireproof gel or a fire suit. There are advantages and disadvantages to each method. Gel is good because it's easy to apply and completely covers the area that will be burned. It isn't bulky as layers of fireproof suits are. It's also more comfortable once the fire is set, because it cools the skin temperature. But gel is expensive, and sometimes it dries out if there's a delay in starting the stunt. Hot camera lights can also dry gel so that it doesn't work as well as it should.

Fireproof clothing is made of a soft material called Nomex. Actually, a suit made of Nomex looks a lot like long underwear. For some stunts, several layers of the suit are worn for extra protection. Every possible opening in the suit is taped tightly shut. The stuntperson has to be careful that flames cannot sneak in through a waistband or armhole and burn his skin.

After the protective material is in place, special effects people paint or spray on some flammable material. They may even add a touch of something like rubber cement. Rubber cement makes a fire smoke, and that looks realistic to the cameras.

Most fire stunts are "partial burns." That means that only part of the body will be set on fire, usually the stuntperson's back. Any part of the front of the body is more risky. Flames could fan up into the face. Fireproof wigs are almost always worn, since human hair can ignite quickly.

"Full body burns" are far more dangerous. The temperature around the body in a full body burn can reach 900° F! Air that hot can't even be breathed. Anyone trying would be killed instantly.

So how *do* they breathe? For full body burns, a special hood is worn. Inside the hood is a bottle

In a full body burn, every second counts.

containing a three-minute supply of oxygen, much like deep-sea divers use. So three minutes is all the time the stuntperson has. Most fire stunts last from 10 to 45 seconds. That seems like a lot of air left over, but remember that the air is used from the moment the stuntperson gets ready for the stunt until the second the fire is put out.

The longer the fire burns, the hotter the temperature inside that suit. Even sweat can be an enemy. It turns to superhot steam, which can cause severe burns! Speed is the name of the game with fire stunts. Every second counts!

WHY BE A STUNTPERSON?

There are, surprisingly, lots of people who try to become stuntpeople. Some are people with a strong background in sports, especially gymnastics. Many newcomers are sons, daughters, or even grandchildren of stuntpeople. That's a real advantage, both in learning how to do stunts and in getting jobs later on. There are even schools run by experienced stuntpeople to train those interested in stunting as a career.

Why be a stuntperson? Certainly not to become famous! The most successful stuntpeople in

Hollywood are not household names. Their fame isn't in the same category with the stars they double for. The movie and television industries want to keep the publicity focused on the stars.

Many stuntpeople say they get satisfaction out of making something hard look easy. They enjoy dressing up in someone else's costume and fooling the audience. Many of them get to travel on location to interesting places. They get to know parts of the world that many people only hear about.

There are qualities that can help someone be a good stuntperson. One important skill is the ability to follow directions—of the director, of the special effects people, even the advice of other stuntpeople.

A good stuntperson is also a good planner and uses

A stuntperson must listen to directions and perform a stunt exactly as it was practiced.

A stuntperson's job is dangerous, but some stuntpeople wouldn't have it any other way!

common sense. Mentally planning a stunt is critical. If a stunt doesn't go as planned, it could not only ruin the filming of the scene, it could endanger the stuntperson's life.

Many stuntpeople owe their success to a healthy body. Most work out several times a week to keep in shape. Staying in shape and limber can help avoid an injury. But, stuntpeople add, a little luck doesn't hurt!

Movies are a great illusion, and stuntpeople are an important part of the work. When they do their job safely, audiences are rewarded with exciting, action-filled movies.

FOR MORE INFORMATION

For more information about stuntmen and stuntwomen write to:

Stuntmen's Association of Motion Pictures
4810 Whitsett Avenue
North Hollywood, CA 91607

GLOSSARY/INDEX

Cage 24—Metal reinforcements around the front seat of a car. A cage makes it less likely that the car will collapse on the driver during a stunt.

Candy glass 18—Fake glass used in movies and television. The glass gets its name from the fake glass made from sugar and hot water in the early days of movies.

Cannon ram 25, 24—A device attached underneath a stunt car. A cannon ram actually "shoots" a pole downward that shoves the car into a roll.

Catcher 23—Anything used to break a stuntperson's fall. Catchers are usually airbags or cardboard boxes.

Full body burn 38—An extremely dangerous stunt where the stuntperson catches fire from head to toe.

Gag 7, 25—What stuntpeople call stunts.

Light gag 17—A stunt that doesn't involve much danger. Fight scenes are considered light gags.

Nomex 38—The material used to fireproof clothing for a stunt.

Partial body burn 38—A fire stunt in which part of the stuntperson's body is set on fire, usually the back.

Props 18—Anything used in a scene to make it realistic. A table, a chair, or glass are all props. Special props, usually made of lighter and safer material, are used for stunts.

GLOSSARY/INDEX

Roll 34, 35 — A stunt that calls for a car to actually "roll" over. Ramps or cannon rams help stunt drivers roll cars.

Roll bar 34 — A metal pole that reinforces the roof of a stunt car.

Running W 15 — A technique, now banned, that was used to trip horses for stunts requiring falls. Many horses were killed because of the Running W.

Special effects advisor 20 — The person in charge of props for a stunt.

Squib 21 — A small explosive charge that is wired to a stuntperson. When the squib is set off, it appears as though a bullet has hit that place.

Talkies 10, 11 — The old-fashioned term for movies that first had sound.

Transfer 13, 14 — A difficult stunt in which a stuntperson switches from one moving object to another — for example, from a galloping horse to a moving stagecoach.